Testimonials

I had the pleasure of working alongside Dean for many years on the set of *The 11th Hour*, which was a daily Christian television program in Northern and Central California as well as Nevada. The Lord used him as our host and guest. He soon became our executive producer. He was requested to speak for many organizations, including FGBMFI (Full Gospel Business Men Fellowship International) meetings. He was a favorite of many men's and women's retreats. He made a major impact on thousands of lives through his many years of service.

He was always being requested to speak …

Sandi Swanson, Producer

The 11th Hour

"Restoring lives one person at a time."

It never ceases to amaze me the people God brings into someone's life. That's the way I see myself when it comes to Dean Wilson, the author of this book. I have known him and his wife, Gayla, for almost forty years. I have watched them go through too many moments and situations in their lives that would have caused some of the strongest Christians I know to consider waving a white flag of surrender.

In his book *Fear: Ten Steps to Victory*, Dean relates personal experiences that have given him a wealth of understanding from a biblical perspective. I have walked alone with him during many of those experiences as a friend and at one time his pastor. We walked many of the same roads together. Dean went from being a host of a local Christian television ministry to being a pastor of a local church. He also knows what's it's like to go through the heartbreak of losing a child. And we both know what it's like to go through a low point in our ministries that cost each of us dearly.

All these issues involved one of the greatest battles every Christian faces: fear. Or more appropriately, a spirit of fear. Fear of how to come back from failure. Fear from wondering if you are doing the right thing. Fear that wants you to quit before you ever get started. Fear at knowing if you're headed the right direction for the Lord. Fear if you even know the right direction.

This book is worth your time.

Rev. Rick Pruitt
Pastor

My first introduction to Dean Wilson was at a ministry meeting. There he was, sitting in a chair with his long ponytail, patiently waiting for prayer. As I touched him to pray for him, the Lord suddenly gave me a word of knowledge for him. For you who don't understand what that is, it's when the Lord reveals something about someone's life to you. It's to help bring direction or confirmation of what the Lord has already been personally speaking to you. I then asked Dean while praying for him, "Are you a bike builder? No wait, not *are* you, but you do build bikes, don't you?" With that wonderful smile of his and that little laugh, he said, "Yes, yes I do." Little did I know at that time our relationship and journey together would begin through this one encounter.

This man, Dean Wilson, whom I was introduced to for prayer, only God himself could have arranged this introduction. It was because of this one introduction, this one encounter, that in the next few years we walked a path together and watched the hand of God himself perform miracles in believers and nonbelievers alike.

It wasn't long after that day I felt like the Lord was instructing me to go to see Dean face-to-face and give him another word. So I did. But this time it wasn't in a church; it was in the parking lot of Back Road Choppers Motorcycle Manufacturing Yard. It was then I knew Dean wasn't only a custom bike builder/manufacturer, but on that day, the Lord also revealed to me that Dean was going to become "Pastor Dean Wilson" of his very own church. So it is not the only place, but yet another place that victory over fear was birthed and delivered. While Dean stepped out in faith and obedience to do what the Lord told him to do, in the natural he struggled with the reality that within his own self, he knew he needed God's help, or he'd fail. After all, he had never been a senior pastor before, and now he was facing yet another level of the fear and insecurity of being a failure like many do in life. But he trusted God. It wasn't long before Pastor Dean by faith gained victory over fear.

I remember relocating to Dean's hometown to help him with his church. I walked into his office one evening just before service. As we sat and talked for a few minutes, Pastor Dean looked across his desk at me and said, "Alan, there's a place beyond faith. There's a place of knowing!" At the time I didn't understand it. Here was a man who had been with the "father of the faith movement," Kenneth Hagin, and now he tells me there's something beyond faith. What did this man have that I needed? I'll tell you what he had; he had a place of knowing!

I went to work with Dean at Back Road Choppers building and selling bikes. Passion, pure passion Dean had for bike-building, but Dean had a level of character that kept him from entering the lifestyle of hard-core bikers, even though he saw them frequently in his shop, at Sturgis, bike shows, and so on.

He lived a life with the fear of the Lord burning in his heart, with a high respect for the Lord. Dean not only had passion, he was saturated with compassion. He constantly encouraged men and women who were struggling with all sorts of issues of life. He would constantly remind them there's more, and there is so much more! Don't give up; don't give in! The only one who can stop you is you!

Dean encouraged me every day by watching him encourage others. At times in his life he was the one who needed the encouragement, yet he gave his life for others.

I truly believe that Dean found the key to survival just like Job. Job was in the middle of this horrific trial in life, yet he wrote, "I know that my redeemer lives" (Job 19:25) NIV. His knowledge of the Lord should serve as a reminder to every believer, bringing hope even in the midst of our trials.

Is this all there is? How many times have I and many of you reading this right now asked, "Is this all there is in life?" I want to remind each of you, like Dean taught me, there's a place beyond faith. It's a place of knowing! As you read this book, I pray your eyes of understanding will be opened to who this man is, Dean Wilson, my friend. He is a real man living a real life in a real world with real struggles, serving a real God from a place of really knowing Him! I often say this when I minister to others, "You can't preach from a field you've never walked in" No, you really can't. So as you read this book, listen closely to the heart of the writer.

There's a saying about the Bible that has a similarity to Dean's book. It goes like this: The blood became ink that the writers wrote it in a book, that we, the readers, as we read the book can take the ink and apply the blood! Dean has learned this. He is an overcomer by the blood of the Lamb and the word of his testimony! He has been to the place of knowing that his Redeemer lives! As you read this book you, too, will visit the place of knowing!

Alan Garren, MM, ThM
Founder and president,
Glory ReVive Ministries, Inc.

FEAR

TEN STEPS TO VICTORY

R DEAN WILSON

WESTBOW
PRESS®
A DIVISION OF THOMAS NELSON
& ZONDERVAN

WestBow Press books may be ordered through booksellers or by contacting:

WestBow Press
A Division of Thomas Nelson & Zondervan
1663 Liberty Drive
Bloomington, IN 47403
www.westbowpress.com
844-714-3454

Scripture taken from the King James Version of the Bible.

Scripture taken from the Amplified Bible, Copyright © 1954, 1958, 1962,
1964, 1965, 1987 by The Lockman Foundation. Used with permission.

ISBN: 978-1-6642-4055-1 (sc)
ISBN: 978-1-6642-4056-8 (hc)
ISBN: 978-1-6642-4054-4 (e)

Library of Congress Control Number: 2021914163

Print information available on the last page.

WestBow Press rev. date: 08/05/2021

CONTENTS

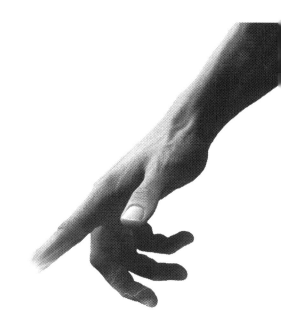

INTRODUCTION

I am excited you have chosen to take this journey with me. My journey began many years ago. As I look back, I would like to tell you it was always easy, and I never failed. But that is simply not the way it happened. When I applied the simple steps I will be sharing with you, I walked in victory. When I did not, I walked in the bondage of fear. Over time, as I witnessed the hand of God moving, when I trusted him it became easier and exciting to be a witness to what he would do.

My prayer is, as you read this book, if you see the simple powerful truths I share with you from the Word of God, your journey will be successful in overcoming the stronghold the enemy has had on your life.

As you read these words, you may feel hopeless. May I encourage you by saying, "There is hope for you." "Faith" is an action word, and by reading this book, you have taken your first and most important step of action against the enemy and one of his greatest tools: fear.

This amazing journey would not be complete

without sharing with you those who God used to make the journey possible.

To my beautiful wife, Gayla, her love and support kept me going forward when I wanted to throw in the towel. For her encouragement in writing this book, thank you will simply never be enough. Only God knows how important you have been. Your encouragement and "stand by your man" attitude have only been made possible because of your steadfast love and faith in God for the impossible to be possible!

To Sandi Swanson, producer of *The 11ᵗʰ Hour* television program that aired for over twenty-eight years in California and Northern Nevada, her unwavering confidence in me was ever present as I moved from a prayer partner to guest on the program and eventually to the host of the program. She also helped me go from being a board member to serving as the president and executive producer of the Christian Foundation.

The exposure to TV media through Christian programming allowed me to be mentored by

Barbara Taylor, aunt to Kenneth Copeland and Jim Sepulveda, who traveled around the globe, sharing the love of Jesus with signs and wonders flowing.

To Chester Smith, owner of Channel 19 television, Ronnie Svenhardt, owner of Svenhardt's Bakery, and many others I will be forever grateful because of the impact they have had on my life.

As the years passed, I served as vice president and president of the local Full Gospel Businessmen Chapter. I also served as elder of our local church, where I frequently ministered the morning Word of God. I also taught the Sunday school class weekly. This was an exciting adventure in itself as I never used a quarterly but simply waited on the Holy Spirit to fill me with the "now" word.

In 2005 my wife and I became very involved in a faith-based drug and alcohol recovery program. Within two years of this experience, the Lord directed us to start a church in a local town close to our home. At this time I was a general contractor, building custom homes in the Central Valley of

California; I also had a motorcycle manufacturing license and was building motorcycles in an 8,000-square foot facility nearby called Back Road Choppers.

Ministering was always at the forefront of my mind. Although I had not given any serious thought to being a pastor, the Lord made it very plain that the call was real. So we ventured out by faith to waters unknown. God blessed, and we saw many come to know the Lord.

We lost our son at age twenty-nine on July 21, 2013. It was only then I realized the impact and the number of lives we had touched for Jesus as we received text messages from around the world.

Some roads we chose, and God blessed other roads we would have much preferred not to have traveled.

My wife received a message many years ago and has been blessed to share it many times: "God has a plan." God has a plan for you if you will only trust him.

Even when trusting in him, I faced the greatest loss a parent could ever face on the earth, the loss of my son, Ryan. I live in the hope and promise of God in my eternal future with him and all his love in heaven.

MY VICTORY
WITH FEAR

I awoke. It was two in the morning, and I was frozen with fear. I could see out through the crack in the bedroom curtains. The moon was shining brightly. I wondered quietly if there would ever be an end to the heartache, confusion, and daily pressure I was living in. As I lay there, the stress became so intense I couldn't remember what it was like *not* to feel this way. For nights, weeks, and months—it seemed like *years*—I had awoke to a growing fear that seemed to be consuming my life.

Thoughts in the past of suicide were now being taken more seriously. As I considered why I had not done so already, the only reason I could hold on to was the love I had for my wife and family.

"The thoughts of someone who does not know God," you say?

No, I was a Spirit-filled Christian coming under the greatest attack Satan could place on my life.

Life Itself

I had allowed every area of my life to receive the scorn of Satan's evil hand. I was now paying the price. The price seemed much too high.

Peace was no longer a feeling. It was simply an empty word. The harder I tried to help myself, the more helpless I became. I finally began to realize I had sunk so deep in depression I couldn't seriously pray; I couldn't talk to God. Though the inner desire of my heart was pure, the presence of God seemed beyond my reach.

My final cry came in the darkness of the night. It was the cry of Peter as he was walking on the water to meet Jesus. And taking his eyes off the Master, he began to sink to a certain death.

Jesus, Save Me

By this time I realized Satan was trying to destroy my life. It had now been about a year since I first knelt on the cold cement of the living room floor and asked God to enter into every area of my life.

Spirit, Soul, and Body

It was a commitment I had never completely made, although I had always loved the Lord, gone to church, and tried to be a good Christian.

At that time the presence of God became so real that just kneeling in his presence was not enough. I soon found myself flat on my face, my whole body trembling as I felt his love, his power from the top of my head to the bottom of my feet.

God's call to me that night was very simple: "Dean, I have not called you to a position. I simply called you to serve. If you will be faithful to serve that which I put before you, I will continue to bless you. And you will see yourself doing things that without my power you could not do."

My response to this call was, "Lord, I will go where you want me to go. I will do what you want me to do. With your help, I will be what you want me to be."

Following this experience came a desire as never before to study God's Word. I had Bibles everywhere, every room of the house, in my car, and in my office, even in restaurants. His Word was with me everywhere.

I began to grow in the Lord. Doors began to open for me to share Jesus with others. Something else was beginning to happen as my desire, commitment, and opportunities begin to open more and more for the things of God. I became aware of an attack from the prince of power of this world, an attack that seemed to increase in direct proportion to my desire and commitment to do God's bidding.

Again, in the darkness of this night, I awoke as I had done so many nights before. Only this time something was different. The fear was there; I had become almost accustomed to this feeling by now. But there was something else, a coldness, almost as though there was a cool breeze blowing down the hall into the bedroom. With the breeze came a chilling heaviness over my entire body. My skin began to feel cold. I felt that Satan himself was in the room to torment and destroy me.

To me, it seemed like hours passed before I decided to wake my wife. To my horror, I discovered I could not move so much as a finger. This frightened me beyond words; I decided since I could not move, I would wake her by calling to her. But I discovered I could not speak either. I felt myself sinking as though into a dark tunnel. My mind was racing almost wildly in helplessness. *What can I do? I cannot move to wake her up. I can't call out for her.*

My mind recalled the woman with the issue of blood. In her simple faith, by simply touching the hem of Jesus's garment, she was healed. Samson, though he had sinned against God, took hold of the two pillars in the temple and asked to feel the power of God just one more time. And Peter's cry on the water, "Jesus, save me."

In the next few minutes I thought back over the temptations, trials, heartaches, and pains of my past. God had never let me down, not one time. I had fallen short many times, but he was always there.

Silently I began to cry out to Jesus, "Save me." As I did so, I began to feel power enter my body, starting at my feet, coming up my legs, up my chest, up my neck, into my thoughts, and almost exploding out of my mouth. "Jesus save me."

Instantly, my skin was warm again, and the heaviness was gone. The cold breeze had vanished. I was once again in his presence. By this time I had awakened my wife, and we rejoiced together over our victory in Jesus.

As the weeks and months passed, God began to show me in his Word how to live an overcoming life of victory, beating fear regardless of the circumstances in my life.

Beloved, God is bigger than all your trials. God is bigger than your heartaches. And God is bigger than any loss you may be experiencing in your life. Just always remember John 10:10 (KJV):

The thief cometh not, but for to steal, and to kill, and to destroy: I am come that they might have life, and that they might have it more abundantly.

ASK YOURSELF

What have I not done because of fear?

Fear of:

- Rejection
- Failure
- What someone else may think
- Inadequacy
- Not enough

Fill in the gaps as it pertains to your life.

Let me say to you, most greatness has gone forth despite fear. In fact, in the very face of fear, let me be so bold as to say if you haven't had to face fear as you look at your dream, then you are not dreaming big enough. God is a big God. If he has given you a dream, he will be there to equip you to fulfill that dream. It is only when you realize you cannot do it that God will say, "I know, son or daughter, that's why I am here. I will help you."

God spoke to me to start a church. The only thing I could see with my naked eyes was a vacant building—in very rundown condition, I might add. We had no waiting congregation, no one to fill the pews, no sound equipment, and no pulpit. Nothing. But my wife and I obeyed what God was leading us to do.

To obey is better than to sacrifice. (Samuel 15:22)KJV

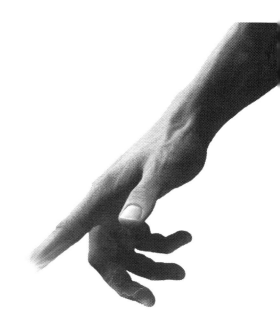

FOLLOW YOUR PASSION

My dad once told me, "Son, find what you love to do, and you will never work a day in your life."

I love motorcycles.

Four wheels are transportation.
Two wheels are a journey.
So go with me on my two-wheel journey.

I bought my first two-wheel scooter at a very young age. I was hooked. I was constantly tinkering on the old Cushman and wondering what it would be like actually to manufacture bikes. As the years passed, that early child's thought was always in the back of my mind.

I was born with an interest in building things. A store-bought wagon wasn't safe in our neighborhood. I would take the wheels off and build a go-cart. I still have a shoebox I made while in grade school. For some, you find that one thing, and it becomes a lifelong season. For others, there may be many seasons to their lives. I am one of many seasons.

Let me share with you some of my seasons. In doing so, I hope to encourage you to embrace the season of life that stands just ahead of you. Remember this: Nothing can stop what God has called you to do except you.

My prayer is that by sharing some of my story it will help you to see how God wants to use you for his purpose. For you to shine where you are, and to give you the courage to move toward where he wants you to shine even brighter. See yourself on a ladder, and every step you take brings you closer to the top, where you can reach out and take the very best God has planned for you. Not your friend, not your pastor, not your neighbor—you. Jim Sepulveda used to say, "There is only one you, so be the best you can be, so He (God) can be the best He can be through you."

At a young age of nineteen, I started a company that built pickup camper shells. A man who worked for me made me an offer to buy the company, and I sold it to him. This was a ten-year journey, and I learned many things about owning and operating my own business.

Following this, my brothers, Evan and Mike, and I started a company, Ride-On Trailers, and built boat trailers.

Following my interest in real estate, I got my real estate license in California. But even then I also enjoyed the exposure it gave me to buy old, rundown houses and fix them up.

Each of these steps was taking me to my early childhood dream of building bikes. I did not know it at the time, but I was only one step away from that dream.

The final step happened in the year 2000, when I got my contractor's license and began to build custom homes. This was very rewarding to me in many ways, including financially. Now the long-suppressed dream of becoming a licensed motorcycle manufacturer resurfaced. I shared that vision with several of my biker friends. All of them said it could not be done.

This is where I need to pause and say to you, "Don't give up your dream because someone tells you it can't be done. If it is a God-given dream, it can happen. Matthew 19:26 tells us with man it is impossible, but with God, all—not some, not a few—but all things are possible.

I am sure someone will read these words and wonder, *how can building motorcycles be a God given dream?* That is the very heart of this book, to first free you from the enemy of fear, and second, to launch you forward to embrace your dream, not your dad's or mom's or your pastor's or even your friend's dreams, but your God-given dream. Stay with me, and maybe you can see through my eyes. I am a big thinker, but God is so much bigger. He never does anything small.

Moses had nothing but a cane in his hand until God touched it. It is never called a cane again but rather a rod. We read in Psalm 23:4 (Amplified), "Your Rod (to protect) your staff (to guide). See what God can do with something as small as a cane?

God is all in. Debra, my eldest daughter, was working for me at the time and caught the vision. She went to work doing what many said couldn't be done, and in less than a year, we were licensed to build and sell motorcycles in all fifty states.

I had the vision. Now I needed someone with the talent, which brings me to my brother Evan. He can make metal do things I didn't think possible. We both had the same vision, build a one-of-a-kind bike, not a knockoff of someone else's. Evan's favorite saying is, "We build bikes to ride, not Easter eggs." And build we did.

We bought three acres with an office, a parts room, and a showroom. There was also a large building for manufacturing our bikes. The site gave us freeway exposure. We hired two men who formally worked at Indian Motorcycle Company. My brother Mike, Ryan, my son, and other family members joined the company along with other employees.

Evan developed three models, and we begin to show. The more shows we attended, the more people who saw our bikes, "Backroad Choppers," the greater the demand.

We soon were receiving calls from major bike

magazines wanting to feature our bikes. We were now going to all the major shows on the West Coast: Laughlin River Run, Bakersfield Bike Fest, Las Vegas Biker Fest, Easy Rider Shows, and more.

In the fall of 2005, we received a call and were asked if we would bring our bikes to Las Vegas, Nevada, to the AMD World Championship V-Twin Custom Bike show. I wondered, *Can this be yet another door God has opened for us?* By now we were well known. We were not going anywhere, like to the after-hour parties. Our standards were different. Let me jump ahead here and say before it was over, we were asked by one of the major bike show promotors if we would hold Sunday morning services for those interested in attending church while at the shows.

Are you getting the message? God will use you many times right where you are planted.

We accepted the invitation to the show. Not only that, Evan said in addition to showing our three production models, he was going to build a bike, one that was outside the box. It was a Pro

Street, low to the ground with a 300 rear tire, 125 horsepower, and a six-speed transmission. This was quite an accomplishment in itself, considering everything else we were committed to. But build it he did.

I remember as if it were yesterday, pulling our enclosed twenty-five-foot trailer into the parking lot of Mandalay Bay, looking around the parking lot at all the big trucks and trailers already there, and wondering, *Is this really a good idea?* It didn't help when I found a place to park, and when getting out of the H-2 Hummer saw I had parked next to the Jessie James Rig. By this time he was well known for his skills both on television and in biker magazines.

But we were there. We unloaded our trailer of bikes and were instructed where to place them in the show.

Some time passed, and one of the promoters of the show stopped and asked if we would enter the Pro Street Evan built in the Custom Free Class category. Why not? We were there, so why not go for it? Still, we were quite intimidated by looking around at all the other bikes and builders there. And again, this was a world trade show, so there were builders from outside the United States.

There was nothing to do now but wait, and then the judging finally began in our category. The first to be announced was honorable mention, then third place and then second place. I caught Evan's eye. We had given it our best shot. So many thoughts were going through my mind that I barely heard over the loud speaker, "And the winner is, Back Road Choppers."

"That's us! We won! Evan, you did it. You did it. Thank you, Jesus." Simply writing these words reminds me of how excited we all were.

So where is the fear in this story? Fear of competing with the big boys! But we had the faith to face the fear.

Someone once said when fear knocks on the front door, send faith to answer, and no one will be there.

Several months later, *Hot Bike* had this Pro

Street as its centerfold bike. And in 2007–2008, we were voted one of the top ten V-Twin motorcycle builders in the United States.

Evan continued to build, redesign, and improve our bikes. The icing on the cake came when Pisano Publishing called and asked if we would be interested in being on the Discovery television network with a special on our company. For one week we had a camera crew at our factory filming what we were doing.

The year 2009 was very busy. We had started the church. More on that later.

Allen Garren, a minister, evangelist, and personal friend, hosted an event at our factory on a Saturday. Many motorcycle ministers, including Jerry Savelle from the Motorcycle Ministry called Chariots of Light in Bakersfield, California, attended. We had food, venders, bike events, and a prayer box, where bikers could write prayer requests. It was a great time of fun, games, and fellowship.

Earlier that year, while showing our bikes at the

Laughlin River Run, we were invited by a man who owned a Main Street property in Sturgis to rent space from him for the upcoming Sturgis rally in August. We took his name and phone number and said we would talk to him later in the year.

He called us several weeks before the rally. The space rent was $20,000. I told him that was not in our budget. A few days passed, and then he called again with an offer of $10,000. I told him that too was not in our budget. The housing market had not been good all year, and there were signs it was going to get worse.

The Friday before the start of the rally, he called again. "If you will come, you can have the space for $5,000. And pay me after the show." This was not an off year for Sturgis. In fact, I learned later that he had turned down several venders in hopes we would come.

We prayed about it and decided to go. Over the weekend we prepared our bikes. Our big rig would carry the bikes plus our clothing line. Monday morning we began loading the trailer.

We had purchased thousands of dollars in inventory earlier in the year. But our dealers, as well as we, were feeling the increased slowing of the housing market, and bike sales were down. Money was really tight.

We needed to leave for Sturgis by day's end to be there by Thursday afternoon. The other vendors could not set up their displays until we pulled into our spot first because of the size of our truck and trailer. The rally was to begin Friday morning.

We had about half the trailer loaded when I told the men to stop. This just did not make any sense. I had been in my office adding up just the cost of diesel fuel. And even with us sleeping in the rig, our wives packing food for the trip, and leaving money in the cash box so business at our showroom could continue while we were gone, there was no room for any kind of breakdown along the way. We had about 1,800 miles ahead of us.

A few minutes passed and Gayla called. She had just received a call from one of our church intercessors, saying, "Tell Dean to go to Sturgis. He will sell every bike he can carry in the trailer."

With that, I told Evan and Mike about the call. "Load the trailer. We are going to the Sturgis Rally."

Later that day we headed for Sturgis. Diesel tanks full for the trip, a prayer, and a promise: 100 percent sellout. I did not have a heavy heart but an excitement at the promise from God.

Mike was the only one licensed to drive this big rig. Evan and I rode in the passenger seat, and the sleeper was behind the cab. This was going to be especially hard for Mike as the truck had to be on the road almost constantly to get there on time.

Everything was going as planned until midday Tuesday. I looked in the rearview mirror and saw smoke coming from under the trailer on the passenger side. Mike knew instantly what had happened; we had a tire failure. We were somewhere in Utah. There was no shoulder to pull on to, but we spotted a building about one mile up the road.

Mike slowed down, and we were able to make it to the pull off. The building turned out to be an adult bookstore. Remember, I told you earlier we were pretty well known by now, and this would not speak well for what we stood for. Many bikers ride their bikes to the rally from California, and there was a steady flow of bikers on the freeway making the long ride. We had a spare tire, and as quickly as we could, we changed tires and were back on our way.

Wednesday morning we took the exit off Interstate 80. We still had a long way to go but were now headed northeast to Sturgis. The road was narrow, more like a country road, not a major freeway. After several hours of driving, our worst fears (Oops, not supposed to be afraid.), the spare tire we put on the trailer blew out. Once again, there was a pull off just ahead, and Mike was able to get both truck and trailer off the road.

We had barely stopped when we heard, "Hey guys, what's the problem?" It was the owner of a retail bike shop in Modesto, only a few miles from our factory. He was on his way to Sturgis just to enjoy the rally. He knew the road well as he had been to the rally several times in the past. "There is a town about twenty miles ahead. Can you make it there with only two tires rather than the three tires on that side of the trailer?" Mike assured him if he drove slowly, we would be okay. "Give me the wheel, and I will take it and have the tire shop there install a new tire." We thanked him, loaded the tire and wheel in his pickup, and off he went.

We still had fuel to buy to take us the final miles to the rally. We all hoped the cost of the new tire would leave us with enough money to buy the necessary diesel. When we arrived at the tire shop a short time later, not only was a new tire mounted on the wheel, but it had been paid for in full! Talk about the favor of God. With renewed faith we were back on the road, making only a short stop, so Mike could get a little rest. We pulled into our reserved spot very early Friday morning.

Yeah, we made it. We were all tired but excited

to be there. We unloaded the trailer of all the bikes and our Back Road Chopper clothing line. We had hats, T-shirts, tank tops, and sweatpants for women. We were ready for business early that Friday morning.

Bikers had been arriving all week, but today was the first official day of business. Now remember, we were here only because of a phone call Gayla received from one of our personnel prayer intercessors who told us we would sell out of everything. It was because of that statement that we decided to go. We could still hear those words ringing in our ears as we readied ourselves for our first big day.

At the end of the first day, which ended around 9 p.m., we had sold three T-shirts. You read it right, three T-shirts. We were at Sturgis and we sell that many T-shirts in our retail store. I was really questioning our decision to come. Little did I know when we finally went to bed around 10 p.m. that it was only going to get worse.

We were awakened around 2 a.m. by a loud

noise and a raging wind. Making a quick exit out of the trailer's sleeping quarters, we were horrified to find our full-length awning that we attach to the side of our trailer at events being shredded to pieces. This was no small thing. I later found out to replace this awning would cost over $8,000.

We went back to bed for a sleepless next few hours, until the sun came up Saturday morning. It was only then that we were able to assess the total destruction of our awning. Not only that, we were the only vender that had sustained any damage. The 10 × 20 pop-up tents were not even damaged. There was now no question in my mind that it was a terrible mistake to go to Sturgis.

I told Evan and Mike if I had the money for fuel to go home we would pack up and go now. This was the lowest of our low. Looking back over our trip there, no sales on Friday, and now the total destruction of our awning. I was done.

But we couldn't go home. I knew that. My sister Karen and her husband, Rick, would be arriving sometime that morning; they were on their way from Texarkana, Arkansas. Karen planned to help out selling our clothing line. It sure did not look like we needed any help with that at this point. So there we were. We decided to make the best of it and see what happened.

Fast-forward to midafternoon on Saturday. Karen was selling our clothing, and we had sold three of the bikes *for cash!* We had a floor safe in our sleeper, but we had more cash on hand than I wanted to put in there. I went downtown, looking for a Bank of America, which is where we had our checking account. The only bank in town was Wells Fargo. I called Gayla and asked her to go to the Wells Fargo in Turlock and open a checking account, and then call me with the numbers. She asked me why, and when I told her I had all this cash and needed to deposit it, she didn't seem all that surprised. Thank the Lord he gave me a wife of great faith.

By the end of Sunday, we had sold 6 bikes for cash. Everyone was paying with cash. Come the following Thursday night, we were 100 percent sold out except for one bike. We had several people wanting the bike but we decided to take it home as something did not sound quite right with the motor. We did not want to sell it until we had more time to check it out.

After returning home, it turned out to be something very simple. And soon after, the bike was sold.

The rally would not be over until Sunday. But we put a sold-out sign on the trailer and spent the balance of our time there meeting other builders and enjoying the rally.

Evan (Master Builder)

I have taken extra time in sharing this story with you. You see, I could have written about the many miracles we witnessed as pastors and directors of two recovery homes. But then many would read this book and say, "Well sure, but you were a pastor. God would to that for a pastor but not for me." And that is my point. God will do abundantly above and beyond for you. Notice that Ephesians 3:20 does not say anything about having to be a pastor. This scripture is speaking directly to you.

My point to this story is to show to you that God is interested in every area of your life. He wants to be a part of everything you do. This may require some "spiritual housecleaning" both to position yourself to hear when he speaks to you, and to be obedient to what he says to do.

Remember, this is of most importance to you receiving total victory in whatever he has promised you. Often what happens between "Amen" and there it is, the road can become very bumpy. Things can in the natural get worse before they get better. Satan will do everything he can to get you to give up before victory comes. I could have thrown in the towel when my sis arrived Saturday morning. Ask for enough money to buy diesel to get home, and we would have never experienced the promise we were given.

As I was writing this last sentence, I visualized someone reading this book. Your mountain seems to be so big that you are feeling hopeless, defeated, and at the point of giving up. Don't quit. If all you can do is stand, then just stand. Victory is yours. Just begin to praise God for the victory that has not manifested in the natural. "It happens in the Spirit before it is seen in the flesh." Praise God all the way to your victory.

NOTHING BUT THE CALL OF GOD: THE CHURCH

Nothing but the call of God. Day after day I drove by the vacant church property on my way to the bank. The weeds were growing where there was once a yard. The paint on the outside walls was peeling and faded. Trash was strewn around the property from lack of care. As I drove by, I would look and then ask God, "Why is your house of worship setting vacant? It is the largest church in this town. Why have you not sent a pastor to pastor this church?

One morning I pulled on to the property, got out of my truck, and looked through the glass doors at the back of the church building. It looked as bad on the inside as it did outside. As I got back in my truck and traveled to the bank, my heart was heavy. As I stopped in the parking lot of the bank, one more time I asked God the same question I had asked so many times before: "God, why have you not sent a pastor to pastor this church?"

As I opened the door and started to step out, I heard a voice in my spirit so loud that I stopped half in the truck and half out. "Dean, I have called a pastor, but he keeps driving by day after day and asking me, 'Why haven't you called a pastor to pastor this church?'" I got back in the truck and begin to weep. And like all the men in the Old Testament, I had all the same excuses: "I'm not good enough." "Who would listen to me?" Excuses, excuses.

TEN STEPS TO
VICTORY

I claim no great revelations, just simple truths I discovered in God's Word.

Let me share with you now some powerful steps you can take that are guaranteed to lead you into a peaceful, victorious, overcoming life in Jesus, free from the destructive powers of fear.

Step 1: When fear suddenly jumps out at you, fear not. Do not panic. (Exodus 14:11)

Moses, inspired by God, instructed his people, "Fear not." Though the situation may in the natural seem a fearful one, God says "Fear not." When you allow fear to take control of your actions, you begin to act negatively. Negative thoughts result in negative actions. God never responded negatively to any situation in his Word. You will not find where God ever says, "Retreat, give up." At the Red Sea, he did not say it was too deep or wait until spring to cross over.

Think outside the box:
What jumps out at you?

When someone jumps out from behind a door and says, "Boo," your first thought might be, *Boy, I was not expecting that.* Well our adversary, the devil, will try his best to catch you off guard, by surprise. For lack of a better word, he ambushes us in the natural, when we're unprepared, like a man going to battle and leaving all his rifle ammunition at home.

Never, never let down your guard. One of our adversary's tricks is to attack you just when you have had some great victory. For example:

- Your son or daughter just committed his or her heart to God.
- A prayer you had been praying for years was answered.
- You got the promotion at work you had hoped for.
- You just moved into the home of your dreams.
- Everything in your life at that moment seems to be perfect.

Step 2: Stand Still

Again, Moses said, "Fear ye not." Stand still, wait, and don't act on your natural response, which is to make a hasty move when the enemy begins his attack. Remember that Satan has had years of experience studying not only your reactions to his attack but those of countless others before you. This time take him by surprise.

> *Think outside the box:*
> *Stand still.*

Do not react in haste. Take time to study the problem from all sides.

Boy, this is a tough one. Everything around me is falling apart, and I am supposed to just stand still? Do not confuse still with not doing anything. This is the perfect time to lock yourself in your prayer closet and seek the Lord. No matter how hopeless it may look, God has the answer. Do not fall into the trap of doing anything and everything you know to do, and when all else fails, then and only then, you go to God.

By this time, like Peter walking on the water to meet Jesus, not having your eyes on Him you will find yourself about to drown. And all this time all you had to do was ask for God's help.

Now do not misunderstand me. God will *always* be there for you. But let me ask you this: Why waste all the time? Go to God first.

Step 3: "For God hath not given us the spirit of fear but of power and of love and of a sound mind" (2 Timothy 1:7) KJV.

Recognize and yes acknowledge if you have fear in your life. Regardless of the reasons, that fear is not from God. The source of all fear is Satan; it is his greatest weapon. The more you operate in fear, the less power and love and peace of mind you will have operating in your life. Remember when you were a child how much fun it was to tease and torment someone who would whine and snivel and get all upset? It wasn't any fun to tease someone who didn't respond.

Remember this when the devil comes against you, and you and will probably react much differently. And Satan may just go elsewhere.

Think outside the box:
Spirit of fear.

The spirit of fear is much different than momentary fear. A car pulls out in front of you, and you apply the brakes on your car, not sure if you can avoid an accident. A spirit of fear never leaves you; it is all-consuming. You cannot shake it off no matter how hard you try. It clouds your mind in such a way it becomes difficult to stay focused and accomplish the simplest task at hand. You hate it. You try to hide from it, you try to run from it, but no matter what you do, it is still over you like a dark cloud.

There is hope for you; there is a way out. You are moving forward at this very moment out from under this dark cloud. Do not quit now. Keep moving forward as you are closer to victory than you know. The last blow from the adversary may have knocked you down, but it did not knock you out. Get up; do not give up. That last blow was meant to take you out. It was his best shot, and by getting up and moving forward, you win over the adversary and he loses.

Step 4: No weapon that is formed against thee shall prosper (Isaiah 54:17) KJV

Repeat this scripture over and over throughout the day. If a fearful thought comes to you, replace it with the Word of God. You cannot think two thoughts at the same time. Repeat it aloud. Satan does not like to hear God's Word, and repeating God's Word will strengthen your faith.

Think outside the box:
Guard your thoughts.

Realize what you are thinking about the adversary will keep you in his power. He will do anything to keep your mind focused on the problem. You may find yourself awake at night, unable to sleep, trying to think about what you should be fearful of. You know there must be something, but what? In your desperation you may find yourself making something up to justify the fear that consumes your every thought. If I am talking to you, know that you are not alone. You are not the only one who has felt this way; this is where I found myself.

I am not writing this based on what someone has told me but from my experiences. This is the reason I am so convinced there is hope for you. God did it for me, and he will do this for you too. He is no respecter of persons. We are all special to him.

Step 5: Walk upright before God (Isaiah 54:14).

In righteousness shalt thou be established? Thou shall be far from oppression for thou shalt not fear.

This is God's promise to you for living a life of righteousness. If you have erred in an area of your life, ask God's forgiveness, and determine in your heart to live a pure life without repeated sin.

Think outside the box:
Examine yourself.

This may be hard to do, but it is an important step in being healed, so do not hesitate. Do it now. It may be something you simply ask God to forgive you of, or you may need to go to someone and ask forgiveness. Some may not receive it as you had hoped for. You have done your part, so now move on. Most important forgive yourself. If you do not, you will carry the guilt with you, and this is not God's plan. Paul, in his writings, says, "This one thing I do, it is my one aspiration forgetting what lies behind." What he is really saying is, "I rid myself of all past guilt." Paul had much more to be forgiven for than you, yet he changed his ways and wrote most of the New Testament.

Step 6: Trust in God's promises (Isaiah 26:3).KJV

Thou will keep him in perfect peace, whose mind is stayed on thee. When the enemy attacks you in any way and you overcome the attack in Jesus's name, write down the victory. Today is the perfect day to start your prayer diary. When Satan attacks you, get out your prayer diary, and read it aloud. Satan doesn't like to hear God's answered prayers, and it strengthens your faith to overcome the present circumstances by remembering what God has already done for you.

Think outside the box:
Think perfect peace.

At this point, perfect peace may seem a far distance from you. Be encouraged, my friend. I promise you it is closer than you think possible.

We find in Matthew 19:26 that with God all things are possible. Not some things, not a few things, but *all* things are possible through him.

Your impossibility has become your possibility because of God in you.

Step 7: God is on your side.

The Lord is on my side, I will not fear. What can man do unto me? (Psalm 118:6)KJV

God is our strength. (Psalm 46:1–2)KJV

Greater is he that is within you than he that is in the world. (1 John 4:4)KJV

> *Think outside the box:*
> *You are not alone.*

According to 2 Timothy 1:7KJV, we are to take hold of God's promises because they were written for us. God never intended for us to live a life under a cloud of fear.

Remember, God did not give you the spirit of fear that has been paralyzing your life. Shake it off by filling your mind with the goodness of God. I promise that you don't half to look very far to see people with many more needs than you. God is on your side. He wants the very best for you. Make a decision today to accept nothing less than the best. God will not do it for you; you must do your part.

As I write these words, I see someone with a lifelong addiction. Your fear is if you sober up long enough, you will have to face all that you have done, all those you have hurt, and all the years you wasted. But the Spirit of God within you would say to you, "Your best days are ahead. It is not too late for you. Your future holds the possibilities of true happiness, joy, and fulfillment." "Take my hand," says the Lord, "and I will help you."

Step 8: Stay in God's Word (Romans 10:17) KJV.

Fear is a spiritual force, just like faith is a spiritual force. So then faith cometh by hearing by the Word of God. Repeat all these promises over and over.

Think outside the box:
Bathe yourself.

Taking a spiritual shower will not get the job done. You need to take a spiritual bath. Soak yourself in his Word. The Word of God is full of promises, and there is a promise that will speak directly to your need.

God commanded Joshua, "Be strong and of good courage be not afraid for the Lord thy God is with thee wherever thou goes" (Joshua 1:9) KJV.

When you place your life under the direction of the Master, past failures need not be final. They can become stepping-stones to success. Say it out loud, "God, I place myself in your hands. I will trust you to bring forth the best in me for your purpose for my life."

Step 9: Be careful what you say.

Omit the word "fear" from your vocabulary. Don't say things like, "I am afraid." Replace words of fear with words of faith in God's ability to see you through. He will.

Think outside the box:
Choose your words carefully.

"Life and death is in the power of the tongue" (Proverbs 18:2) KJV. That is a powerful statement. I like to put it this way:

- Change your thoughts.
- Change your talk.
- Change your life.

It all starts with your thoughts. Guard what you think about. If you think about fear, that is what your life will be. So change your perspective.

Think about faith, and fear will have no choice but to leave. Both faith and fear are spiritual forces. Faith is from God. Fear is from your adversary. You can't think about faith and fear at the same time. Faith will overpower your fears if applied.

It has been said that "There is nothing to fear but fear itself."

Step 10: Remember, if you slip, do not become discouraged.

Get up and try again. When you joined hands with Jesus, he didn't join your team. You joined his team, and he always wins. That means you win. You can do it; God does not make any failures. You only fail if you give up. Determine now that you will be an overcomer in the name of Jesus.

Think outside the box:
You blew it, so what?

The Bible says we have all came short, and no one is without sin.

A story is told of a little boy who was afraid to walk alone in the darkness. But when his father walked beside him and took his hand, all fear vanished. The darkness now held no fear because he loved and trusted his father, and the little boy knew he would take care of him.

Here is the key for us to be free from fear: We must learn to know our heavenly father well. As we become acquainted with God, we trust our lives completely to him. Placing our hands safely in his, we humbly ask him the questions that plague our minds and about those sorrows of life that would drive us to despair.

May I encourage you today to take hold of Jesus's hand? His is outstretched for you to take hold.

My son wrote on the inside back cover of my Bible these words on the last day of his life on earth:

You're not waiting on God.

God is waiting on you.

This will be the most important step you will ever take in your life.

May God richly bless you on your own journey.

IS THIS ALL
THERE IS?

You may find yourself at a place in your life when he has used you in some powerful way. And now the season has changed. You are not being used in his work as you once were, and so the question is, "Is this all there is?"

I write these words out of my own life experiences. God—because of your abundant grace, love, goodness—my life has been full. You have used me in ways I could have never imagined. I was blessed to be mentored by Jim Sepulveda and many more.

Doors simply opened in front of me. I simply have and had a burning desire to be used by God for the lost and hurting.

But God, I am still here. What now? I am still alive, so you must still have a plan, something that could only happen with your help, something I could not do without you, something that could touch more people with the love of God.

This book began to come together in my spirit. My earnest prayer is as you have read the simple highlights of my life, God will have spoken to you. You will follow the ten steps and be free from the bondages of fear. You will once again stir up the dream deep within you. The pilot light it still burning; turn on the burner in your spirit.

I have been accused of living right on the edge. I take that as a compliment. Nothing happens unless you start moving forward to the passion and dream in your heart. The Lord once spoke to me these words, "Son, I have not blessed your sets I have blessed your steps" (Psalm 37:23). Take a step of faith today, and see what God will do that you alone cannot do.

I AM A WINNER

Fear	Faith
You can't.	I can.
You won't make it.	Never give up.
It's over.	It's not over.
There's no use.	There is hope.
You're a loser.	I am a winner.
You will never beat.	I am already beating.
The addiction.	The addiction.
You took the wrong road.	I have been given a new road map; I am on the right road.
I will keep planting thoughts of fear and failure in your mind.	Shut your dirty mouth.

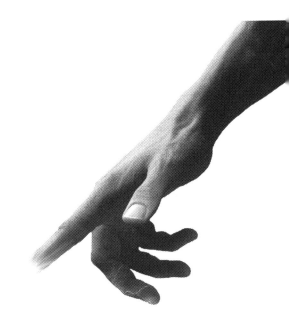

INTRODUCTION TO THE SINNER'S PRAYER

Your loving heavenly Father has a special plan for your life. His promise to never leave or forsake you is unconditional. When Jesus died on the cross, it secured the best life you can live through him on earth as well as secured your everlasting home in heaven. If you have never prayed the sinner's prayer, pray it now. When you pray this simple prayer, see the stamp in your hand placing it on your very own spiritual envelope. Welcome, my friend, to God's family.

When I was the pastor and director for the men's recovery home, I often gave them this visual picture. Disconnect your umbilical cord from whatever addiction you have and place it into Jesus. The power of the Holy Spirit will now infuse your very being, Spirit, soul, and body.

THE SINNER'S
PRAYER

1. *Romans 3:23 KJV*
   States, All Have Sinned

2. *Romans 5:15 KJV*
   States, Salvation Is a Gift

Jesus, I come to you a sinner. I ask you to forgive me of all my sins. I receive you as my Lord and Savior. Thank you, Lord Jesus, for your death on the cross that I may be cleansed by your blood and have life eternal.

SCRIPTURES FOR
A FULL LIFE

God hath not given us a spirit of Fear but of Power and Love and a sound mind. (2 Timothy 1:7) KJV

I can do all things through Christ who strengthens me. (Philippians 4:13) KJV

The Lord is on my side. (Psalm 118:7 Amplified Bible)

Thou will keep him in perfect peace, whose mind is stayed on Thee. (Isaiah 26:3) KJV

Yea, though I walk through the valley of the shadow of death, I will Fear no evil. (Psalm 23:4) KJV

I will instruct you and teach you in the way you should go. (Psalm 32:8) KJV

If they obey and serve him they shall spend their days in prosperity and their years in pleasures. (Job 36:11) KJV

Rejoice not against me oh my enemy when I fall, I shall arise. (Micah 7:8) KJV

For I know the plans I have for you declares the Lord, plans to prosper you and not to harm you. (Jeremiah 29:11) NIV

And he said, the things that are impossible with me are possible with God. (Luke 18:27)KJV

Peace I leave with you, my peace I give unto you, not as the world giveth, give I unto you. Let not your heart be troubled neither be afraid. (John 14:27) KJV

Know in all these things we are more than conquerors through him who loved us. (Romans 8:37) KJV

Finally, my brethren, be strong in the Lord, and in the power of his might. (Ephesians 6:10) KJV

Brethren, I count not myself to have apprehended, but this one thing I do, forgetting those things which are behind and reaching forward to what lies ahead. (Philippians 3:13) KJV

So their faith comes by hearing, and hearing be the word of God. (Romans 10:17)

A MESSAGE
FROM GAYLA

Let me tell you about R. Dean Wilson and why you should read this book.

Dean is a man who, though imperfect, never gives up. He's my Eveready Battery; he just keeps on chugging. He was raised on a dairy with two younger brothers and a younger sister. Everything the boys looked at they pictured a motor on it. So they tried to push one of them down a hill, or pulled an old, old car out of a gully and worked and worked on it until Daddy said, "That's enough."

When I met Dean he had moved to Modesto and was a real estate broker. We would buy old houses, fix them up, and resell them. Interest rates skyrocketed, and then we couldn't give a house away.

I talked him into taking a day off, which rarely happened. When we took the off-ramp into town, to the left was our home, and to the right was our real estate office. He was always stopping at the office to check his messages, even if it was midnight. But surprisingly, this time he turned toward home. I asked him why he wasn't going to check his messages, and he stated he just felt that he should go home.

As we walked into the house, the phone was ringing. It was the fire department inspector telling us our office was on fire. He said if we had opened the front door, the place would have exploded outward, fried Dean's lungs, and probably killed anyone in the car. We figured God must have had a plan for our lives.

One day we were praying, "How can we help you, Lord." We had no money, and God told us to tithe our time. So Dean offered to pick up a speaker for our church and take him anywhere he needed to go. Just so happened it was *The 11ᵗʰ Hour*, which was a live Christian television ministry in California and Nevada. That started us going out and praying for people on the phone. One time the guest didn't show, so the host—who was a six feet six inches tall and a really big man took his jacket off and put it on Dean. It was way too big. He tucked in the sleeves and paper clipped the back of the jacket. Dean was now the guest. Dean told about the fire. Later he was asked to guest and host. Eventually he became president and executive producer. God's promotion, not man's. That started years and years of television ministry for both of us. We have been on the mountaintops and in the trenches as well.

Our only son was going to turn sixteen, and our daughters were older. When each one got their drivers' licenses, they also got their motorcycle licenses as we rode as a family everywhere we went. So Dean and Ryan started building a motorcycle in the garage as he neared his sixteenth birthday. They worked on it for months and months. And when they finished, people started inquiring if we could build one for them as well. So we built another and then another and then another. Pretty soon the garage looked like a bike shop.

One day I woke up. And there was a man outside the kitchen window. I told Dean, "That is it. You have to have your own space." so I set out to find a place for Back Road Choppers. Of course four years into this, fully licensed as a manufacturer and going full throttle, the market crashed, and you couldn't give a bike away.

In the middle of the crash, God told Dean to start a church and even gave him the church. I thought he must of have been smoking something, and that is what I told him. (Even though he doesn't smoke anything.) He kept going by this church on the way to the bank and asking God why he didn't send someone to pastor this church. One day God spoke to his spirit. And as Dean shared earlier in the book, Dean was that someone. He called me and told to get a key for the church, and lo and behold, a week later a pastor friend of ours called and said "Gayla, I really feel the Lord is telling me that you and Dean need to be ordained."

My response was, "Not you too." Needless to say, we were ordained and pastored for ten years at New Life International Ministries in Delhi, California. God had a plan.

Then our son drowned, and I lost it. And my heart did likewise.

Dean my Eveready Battery just kept on chugging.

But inside he was just as devastated as I was. That was eight years ago. The man never gives up; he just adapts. A common man, not perfect but that man has stickability!

Eventually we closed the church, and here we are, senior citizens, and asking, "Is that all there is, Lord?" God said to write a book.

"Captain"
Master of his Home

ABOUT THE
AUTHOR

R. Dean Wilson lives in central California with his wife, Gayla, Sister Karen, and Gayla's mother, Sharlene. They all call her mom.

Our family also includes our St. Bernard, Captain, doesn't know he is a dog. He's simply a family member. Boxer, Karen's  dog, I call Hoover because he follows Captain around cleaning any small crumbs Captain drops on the floor when eating treats. And last of all, Maggie, our bird. Her cage is by the front window, and she is the alarm clock or doorbell, letting everyone in the house know when she sees my pickup pull in front of the house.

Dean can be reached by mail at:

Dean Wilson

PO Box 58

Denair, CA 95316

(wwilsonfam@aol.com)

Printed in the United States
by Baker & Taylor Publisher Services